What Is The Bible?

Understand Its History, Find Personal Meaning, and Connect With Its Author

Jack Wolf

POSG Inc

Contents

Chapter One

Introduction: The Journey Begins

Imagine this: every second of every day, about 63,000 searches are typed into Google, adding up to a mind-boggling 5.6 billion queries daily[1]. The whole world is huddled around a giant campfire, sharing stories and asking questions. And in this global conversation, a fascinating trend emerges, especially in the realm of faith and spirituality. One question frequently pops up among the countless topics that pique people's curiosity: "What is the Bible?" In 2022, people worldwide searched this simple yet profound question about 1,000,000 times monthly on Google[2]. It seems increasingly clear that people everywhere are eager to peel back the layers of this ancient book.

So, why a book on the Bible, you might ask? Well, it's not just any book we're talking about. The Bible is a mosaic of tales and teachings that have been a bedrock of cultures, a muse for artists, and a compass for the faithful. It's a storybook, a history lesson, and a spiritual guide all rolled into one. In this book, we're setting off on an adventure to explore this timeless text – its past, its message, and the mysterious Author behind its words.

Our journey starts by diving into the history of the Bible. It's like opening a time capsule filled with ancient writings that span centuries.

We'll discover how this collection of diverse books came to be and how each chapter and verse found its place in the grand narrative. But this exploration isn't just about dates and authors; it's about connecting the dots to our lives today.

Then, we're going to get personal with the Bible. How does this ancient book resonate in the modern world? In a time when personal stories and experiences are cherished, we'll see how the Bible's age-old lessons still echo in our hearts and minds. We'll meet people who find comfort, guidance, and even a bit of themselves in its pages.

And, of course, we can't talk about the Bible without talking about its Author. This subject has intrigued and inspired millions. This part of our journey is about exploring that divine connection and understanding how the faithful view and interact with this sacred text as the living word of God.

But people haven't always viewed the Bible from the same vantage point. We'll see how the Bible has been understood in different times, cultures, and contexts. It's like chatting with many interesting folks, each sharing their unique take on this timeless book.

The journey to understand and connect with the Bible isn't for the devout or the scholarly. It's a journey for anyone who's ever wondered about the Bible, whether out of faith, curiosity, or a love for stories that have stood the test of time. We'll dig deep but keep it light and engaging, like a good talk with an old friend.

So, grab your favorite chair, pour yourself a cup of something nice, and let's embark on this journey together. Through the pages of this book, we'll explore, question, and find a few answers. Welcome to the fascinating, complex, and ever-relevant world of the Bible. Let's start this adventure.

Chapter Two

The Roots of the Scripture

A personal journey from the Author's experience with the Bible

The Bible has been many things to me personally. First, it has been a love story unfolding, with me as the recipient. Second, it has been a guide, helping me know and adapt to the heart of God. Third, it has been an instruction manual, teaching me how to live in freedom and goodness. We will explore these concepts later.

But the week I met Jesus, I was five years old. I attended a presentation every day for five days at a friend's house. During this presentation, I listened to a disabled Vietnam War veteran in a wheelchair tell the story of Jesus as described in the first four books of the New Testament. Each day, he ended with the same question.

"Would anyone like to pray to ask Jesus to reveal himself to you and to live in your heart forever?"

I would go to the kitchen with him each day to pray the same prayer.

"Jesus, thank you for dying for me, as the Bible says. Please come into my life."

On the final day, this broken war veteran asked me why I kept coming forward to pray the same prayer when I only needed to do it once. I replied, "I want to be closer to Him." My heart burned as I longed to know the One who seemed so close yet unknowable.

And that is the entire point of the Bible: to describe and reveal Jesus to humanity so that we can find Him and be closer to Him. He loves us so much and wants to be close to us.

John 3:17 tells us, "God sent His Son into the world not to judge the world, but to save the world through Him."[3]

In John 15:11-16, Jesus explains, "I have told you these things so that you will be filled with My joy. Yes, your joy will overflow! .... There is no greater love than to lay down one's life for one's friends. You are My friends if you do what I command. I no longer call you slaves, because a master doesn't confide in His slaves. Now you are My friends, since I have told you everything the Father told Me. You didn't choose Me. I chose you. I appointed you to go and produce lasting fruit, so that the Father will give you whatever you ask for, using My name."

Jesus not only wants to be close to us, but He also cares about overflowing the joy in our lives and helping us to learn how to ask God to help us in our times of need. We would know none of this if we didn't have the Bible to reveal these concepts to us. With His heart in mind, we dive into the history and development of the Bible. I hope you find the same love-sickness and longing to know Him I have discovered as I explore it.

The Historical Influence of the Bible

The influence of the Bible on major historical events and cultural developments is extensive and profound. Here are some key areas where the Bible has played a significant role:

1. **Legal and Moral Codes**: The Bible's teachings, such as the Ten Commandments, have shaped Western societies' legal and moral frameworks. Concepts like "thou shalt not steal" or "love thy neighbor" have been integrated into laws and societal norms, establishing a foundation for right and wrong.

2. **Arts and Literature**: The Bible has tremendously impacted the arts.

Countless paintings, sculptures, songs, and stories reference Bible stories or characters. Biblical narratives directly inspire iconic works like Michelangelo's Sistine Chapel and Handel's Messiah. In literature, the Bible's influence is evident in works like John Milton's "Paradise Lost" and C.S. Lewis's "The Lion, the Witch, and the Wardrobe," where biblical themes and characters are prominently featured.

3. **Education and Intellectual History**: Historically, the Bible was one of the few available books, making it a primary resource for learning to read and write. This tradition continues today with the study of the Bible

in various educational contexts. The Bible has also sparked significant intellectual thought, influencing philosophy, theology, and history. Its narratives have raised crucial questions about morality, existence, and the divine, stimulating philosophical and theological debates.

4. **Social Justice and Ethical Teachings**: The Bible emphasizes justice and helping those in need, with stories and parables advocating for the poor, the oppressed, and the pursuit of justice. These teachings have inspired many social justice movements and charitable organizations throughout history.

5. **Cultural Influence**: The Bible's stories, characters, and symbolism have left an indelible mark on Western culture. Biblical references are prevalent from classical compositions to modern pop songs. The Bible's powerful stories and symbolic language have influenced Western storytelling's narrative structures and themes, such as redemption, sacrifice, and the battle between good and evil.

The Bible's influence on history and culture is far-reaching, impacting legal systems, arts, literature, education, social justice, and societies' moral and ethical foundations[4].

The Bible's universal appeal and diverse interpretations.

The Bible's universal appeal and diverse interpretations are rooted in its rich, complex narratives and profound moral teachings, which resonate with a wide variety of cultures and individuals worldwide.

1. **Cultural and Historical Contexts:** Different cultures interpret the Bible through the lens of their own experiences and histories. This leads to diverse understandings of its messages.

2. **Theological Perspectives:** Various Christian denominations and Jewish traditions interpret the Bible differently, leading to a spectrum of theological beliefs and practices.

3. **Literary and Symbolic Interpretations:** The Bible's literary qualities, such as parables and metaphors, allow for multiple layers of interpretation, making it relevant to different times and places.

4. **Personal Relevance:** Individuals find personal meaning in the Bible, applying its teachings to their own lives in unique ways.

5. **Scholarly Analysis:** Scholars study the Bible from historical, linguistic, and cultural perspectives, contributing to its diverse interpretations.

The Bible's ability to be interpreted in various ways contributes to its enduring appeal, making it a significant and influential text across different societies and throughout history.

Overview of the book's purpose and structure

The history of the Bible is also a complex and fascinating journey that spans several millennia and involves a wide array of cultures, languages, and religious traditions in its makeup. Here's an overview:

Origins and High-Level Composition

Early Texts: The Bible's origins trace back to ancient oral traditions. The earliest written components, which may have emerged around the 12th century B.C.E., aren't entirely known. However, the Bible describes written laws, historical written collections, and songs from much earlier, leading us to believe that the people who lived much earlier were indeed writing their experiences, which are now included in the overall books within the Bible.

Hebrew Bible (Old Testament): The Old Testament is the first half of the Bible. It is composed of 39 books. This part of the Bible was primarily written in Hebrew, with some parts in Aramaic. It includes the Torah (the first five books), the Prophets, and the Other Writings. The process of its composition and compilation extended from before the 12th century B.C.E. to the 2nd century C.E.

The Old Testament shows us the world's creation, the introduction of sin, and the fall of man from the perfection of living in closeness with God (often described as "paradise" in popular terms). It continues with God putting into action a plan to reserve a people for Himself to steward a lifestyle of closeness with Him. This covenant lifestyle would be signified and stewarded by traditions, sacrifices, and laws, pointing to the need for a one-day coming savior who would return humanity to the fullness of all that was lost to sin.

God moves through unlikely heroes and flawed underdogs throughout the Old Testament. This shows that no matter how imperfect or unlikely anyone may be, God would embrace humanity and lead them toward His ultimate plan to restore all things and set right what was made broken, perverted, and wrong by the introduction of sin and the selfishness that follows.

Here are how the Old Testament books are organized in the Bible:

BOOKS OF THE LAW: These five books cover the laws of God. They begin with the story of Creation and move through the early years of the founding fathers of the Israelite people, and the laws that both governed and uniquely set them apart compared to other nations or peoples on earth.

Genesis

Exodus

Leviticus

Numbers

Deuteronomy

HISTORICAL BOOKS: These twelve books cover the time period of approximately 1400 BC to approximately 500 BC.

Joshua

Judges

Ruth

First Samuel

Second Samuel

First Kings

Second Kings

First Chronicles

Second Chronicles

Ezra

Nehemiah

Esther

POETRY BOOKS: These books are collectively labeled as poetry to describe how each uniquely conveys its thoughts.

Job

Psalms

Proverbs

Ecclesiastes

Song of Solomon

MAJOR PROPHETS: The following 17 books, listed in the these two sections, cover prophetic messages given as a warning to people, who were living in rebellion to the Lord. The messages layout how the people could return to the Lord and predicted future outcomes, many of which happened later in time. The words "major" and "minor" are used to describe the size of the books, not the significance of the prophets within these books.

Isaiah

Jeremiah

Lamentations

Ezekiel

Daniel

MINOR PROPHETS:A description of this section is shared with the "Major Prophets" section above.

Hosea

Joel

Amos

Obadiah

Jonah

Micah

Nahum

Habbakuk

Zephaniah

Haggai

Zechariah

Malachi

New Testament: Roughly 400 years passed between the end of the Old Testament and the opening events of the New Testament, beginning with the birth of Jesus. It is written in Greek and consists of 27 books: the Gospels (stories of Jesus), Acts of the Apostles, Epistles (letters), and Revelation. The composition of these texts occurred between approximately 50 C.E. and 110 CE in the context of early Christian communities.

While the Old Testament points to the one-day need for a Savior. The New Testament opens by introducing us to the Savior. It ends by pointing back to the finished work of Jesus and the unfolding of His rescue plan catalyzed by His death and resurrection for humanity.

The New Testament ushers in the New Covenant mediated between God and humanity by Jesus, the Son of God, also known as Jesus Christ: the Anointed One (A.K.A. "Messiah"). The introduction of this New Covenant was made possible when Jesus lived a perfectly sinless and spotless life, was crucified on a cross for the sins of the world, and rose again from the dead three days later, as He and the Scriptures predicted. This New Covenant makes closeness with God possible, not by traditions, sacrifices, and laws, but by receiving Jesus' death and resurrection as the final atonement for our wrongdoings. He took the punishment for us and set us in right standing with God. All of this, of course, was motivated by His relentless and limitless love for humanity in calling them back into His plan of restoration to perfection.

Romans 5:6-11 tells us, "When we were utterly helpless, Christ came at just the right time and died for us sinners. Now, most people would not be willing to die for an upright person, though someone might perhaps be willing to die for a person who is especially good. But God showed His great love for us by sending Christ to die for us while we were still sinners. And since we have been made right in God's sight by the blood of Christ, He will certainly save us from God's condemnation. For since our friendship with God was restored by the death of His Son while we were still His enemies, we will certainly be saved through the life of His Son. So now we can rejoice in our wonderful new relationship with God because our Lord Jesus Christ has made us friends of God."

Here is the topical layout of the 27 New Testament books:

GOSPELS: These four books tell of the life, death, and resurrection of Jesus Christ, the Messiah

Matthew

Mark

Luke

John

HISTORY: There is only one book in this section. It tells of the history of the early church. It is called "The Acts of the Apostles" and may also be more casually known as "Acts"

EPISTLES: The word "epistle" means "letter" in the early Greek language. These 21 letters were written to difference churches, gatherings, or people.

Romans

First Corinthians

Second Corinthians

Galatians

Ephesians

Philippians

Colossians

First Thessalonians

Second Thessalonians

First Timothy

Second Timothy

Titus

Philemon

Hebrews

James

First Peter

Second Peter

First John

Second John

Third John

Jude

PROPHECY: The final book of the New Testament is called "Revelation" in abbreviated form. Its unabbreviated name is "The Revelation of Jesus Christ". It tells of the final steps to God's plan to bring the world back to the perfection of closeness with Him. It includes many mysterious concepts of future war, famine, and "tribulation." During this phase, God will bring all that is unwaveringly evil and opposed to Him to its conclusion. He will draw out the vial and evil of humanity and the demonic realm, along with the devil and demons, into one final conflict, where hard battle lines are drawn. Evil is defeated once and for all.

Jesus tells us that He will return for us one day and restore us to perfection on the earth for all eternity. So we look forward to His return, as we live every day in the hope and reality that He might come for us any day soon.

The historical context in which the Bible was written

The historical context of the Bible is diverse and spans several centuries, involving different cultures and empires. Here are vital aspects:

1. **Early Israelite history (1200-500 B.C.E.):** Parts of the Old Testament were written during this period, reflecting the history and culture of the ancient Israelites. This era includes their formation as a people, the establishment of the kingdom of

Israel, and later, the division into the kingdoms of Israel and Judah.

2. **Babylonian Exile (6th Century B.C.E.):** Many of the Hebrew Bible's texts, especially those concerning themes of exile and return, were likely compiled or edited during or after the Babylonian Exile.

3. **Persian and Hellenistic Periods (539-323 B.C.E.):** Following the return from exile, the Jewish community was under Persian, then Greek control. This period saw the final compilation of much of the Hebrew Bible and reflects a blend of Jewish tradition with Persian and Hellenistic influences.

4. **Roman Period (1st Century C.E.):** The New Testament was written in the context of the Roman occupation of Judea. It reflects the social, political, and religious struggles of the time, including the emergence of Christianity from its Jewish roots.

The Bible thus encapsulates a wide range of historical, political, and cultural contexts, making its texts rich and multi-layered.

The process of canonization and different versions of the Bible

Canonization refers to determining which materials should be considered part of the Bible and which should not. The process of the canonization of the books of the Bible involved the selection and recognition of specific texts as authoritative and sacred. This process varied for the Hebrew Bible (Old Testament) and the New Testament.

1. **Hebrew Bible (Old Testament):** The canonization of the Hebrew Bible was a gradual process, concluding around the 2nd century C.E. It involved the recognition of the Torah, the Prophets, and the Writings as sacred Scripture by the overall Jewish community.

2. **New Testament:** The New Testament canon was formed over several centuries. Early Christian communities used various texts, but until the 4th century, the current 27 books were widely accepted and influenced by church councils and leaders.

3. **Different Versions of the Bible:**

- **Septuagint:** A Greek translation of the Hebrew Bible, important in early Christianity.

- **Latin Vulgate:** A critical Latin translation by St. Jerome in the 4th century, widely used in the Western Church.

- **Protestant Bibles:** After the Reformation, Protestant versions omitted the Deuterocanonical books in Catholic Bibles.

- **Eastern Orthodox Bibles:** Include additional books not found in Protestant or Catholic canons.

These versions reflect linguistic, theological, and cultural differences in how communities have interacted with and understood the Bible.

How historical events have shaped the Bible's narrative

Historical events have significantly shaped the Bible's narrative:

1. **Exodus and Conquest**: The story of the Exodus and the conquest of Canaan formed the foundation of Israelite identity and faith.

2. **Babylonian Exile**: These events, which took place during the Babylonian and Assyrian empires, profoundly influenced the themes of loss, hope, and restoration in the

Hebrew Bible, particularly in the Prophets and Psalms.

3. **Roman Occupation**: The New Testament reflects the social, political, and religious context of Roman-occupied Judea during the period known as the Roman Empire, influencing the themes of messianic expectation, suffering, and salvation.

These events shaped the Bible's content, interpretation, and significance within Jewish and Christian traditions.

Chapter Three

The Bible in Your Life

I remember the day that I was reading the Bible as a teenager. I read Psalm 139, where the writer tells the Lord, "You made all the delicate, inner parts of my body and knit me together in my mother's womb. Thank You for making me so wonderfully complex! Your workmanship is marvelous—how well I know it. You watched me as I was being formed in utter seclusion, as I was woven together in the dark of the womb. You saw me before I was born. Every day of my life was recorded in Your book. Every moment was laid out before a single day had passed. How precious are Your thoughts about me, O God. They cannot be numbered! I can't even count them; they outnumber the grains of sand! And when I wake up, You are still with me!"

Somehow, I knew this conversation was for me. I felt as if God told me, "I love you, and I find all your thoughts so precious and near to my heart."

I told my mother, "I believe God told me today that Psalm 139 is mine. He loves me and has so many good thoughts about me that I could never count the number if I tried!"

She replied with an expected, "That's nice, dear."

But I could tell that she wasn't convinced. She didn't want to discourage me with a disappointing view of reality. The next day, she attended a prayer meeting at her church. One of the older women said to her, "I believe I heard the Lord tell me that Psalm 139 is for your son. This is his Psalm!"

My mother almost fell over. Could it be true? Does God really reveal Himself so intimately through the Bible? Or does He give us history, context, and allegory?

How to interpret biblical teachings in a contemporary context

With this overall concept that God can use the Bible to speak to us directly, how do we know when and how to interpret Scripture directly spoken to us versus indirectly for historical purposes? Interpreting biblical teachings in a contemporary context involves the following simultaneous tools and perspectives:

1. **Understanding Historical Context**: Recognizing biblical texts' historical and cultural settings can provide insights into their original meanings.

2. **Analyzing Literary Forms**: Differentiating between various literary genres in the Bible, such as poetry, narrative, and prophecy, aids in appropriate interpretation.

3. **Applying Ethical and Moral Principles**: Extracting timeless ethical and moral teachings from the Bible and applying them to contemporary issues and personal conduct.

4. **Engaging with Theological Perspectives**: Considering various theological viewpoints helps in comprehending the diverse interpretations of biblical teachings.

5. **Personal Reflection and Application**: Reflecting on how biblical teachings resonate with unique, personal experiences and societal challenges today.

6. **Seeking Diverse Interpretations**: Consulting different interpretations and commentaries can broaden understanding and avoid narrow readings.

7. **Balancing Tradition and Modernity**: Navigating between

traditional understandings and contemporary perspectives to find relevance in the modern world.

This approach allows for a respectful and thoughtful engagement with biblical texts, making them applicable and meaningful in today's context. However, we should always maintain the fact that Jesus told the religious leaders of His day in John 5:39 "You search the Scriptures because you think they give you eternal life. But the Scriptures point to Me!"

Ultimately, the Bible tells how Jesus entered our broken, dark world to rescue and restore us to perfection and life. Whether examining a Scripture or its historical context, moral principle, or personal application, we must never forget that Jesus is pursuing us and revealing Himself throughout the Bible.

The role of the Bible in moral and ethical decision-making

Besides revealing the love of God through the story of Jesus, the Bible also plays a significant role in moral and ethical decision-making for many people:

1. **Source of Moral Teachings:** It offers ethical guidelines, such as the Ten Commandments and the teachings of Jesus, which many use as a moral compass.

2. **Framework for Ethical Reflection:** The Bible provides narratives and parables encouraging reflection on complex moral issues.

3. **Influence on Laws and Social

Norms: Biblical principles have historically influenced laws and societal norms, shaping concepts of justice, compassion, and human rights.

4. **Guidance in Personal and Community Ethics:** For believers, the Bible guides personal behavior and community interactions, informing choices and actions.

Overall, the Bible is a foundational text for many in shaping their understanding of right and wrong, informing both individual and collective ethical decisions. In the United States court system, we still place our hands on the Bible as we promise to tell the truth. This reminds us that the Bible was meant to reveal truth to humanity because it reveals the One who authored truth, speaks only the truth, and loves when His people live in truth.

Understanding the personal relevance of the truth of the Bible often leads to a deeper exploration of its spiritual essence:

1. **Personal Reflection:** Engaging with the Bible personally can prompt individuals to reflect on their own beliefs and values, leading to a deeper spiritual understanding.

2. **Connecting with Themes:** Identifying with the universal themes in the Bible, such as love, forgiveness, and redemption, can enhance spiritual growth and insight.

3. **Spiritual Practice:** Reading and contemplating biblical texts can

become a spiritual discipline, fostering a deeper connection with God, the Author.

This process of personal engagement with the Bible provides individual meaning and opens pathways to understanding its broader spiritual messages.

Chapter Four

A Spiritual Guidebook

Brother Andrew, known as "God's Smuggler," experienced a profound spiritual awakening that deeply intertwined with his engagement with the Bible. His journey began strikingly: after being wounded as a soldier for the Netherlands military in Indonesia, he found faith during his rehabilitation by reading a Bible. This moment of spiritual awakening transformed him, leading him to dedicate his life to a unique mission: smuggling Bibles to persecuted

Christians behind the Iron Curtain during the Cold War.

One notable instance that highlights the impact of his mission occurred during a trip to Yugoslavia. Bill Bathman, recalling a conversation with Brother Andrew in 1966, learned about Andrew's plan to publish his testimony under the title "God's Smuggler." This book would later play a significant role in raising global awareness about the plight of persecuted Christians in Eastern Europe under communist regimes. While Brother Andrew's work was fraught with dangers, his decision to share his testimony and experiences demonstrated the powerful influence of the Bible not only on his life but also on the broader context of religious freedom and spiritual resilience during a tumultuous historical period.

Brother Andrew's life story is a compelling example of how spiritual awakening through the Bible can lead to impactful actions and profound changes, both personally and in the broader world. His journey from a wounded soldier to a dedicated missionary reflects the transformative power of biblical teachings and their significant role in shaping one's life purpose and actions[5].

The Bible as a source of spiritual guidance and comfort

The Bible serves as a significant source of spiritual guidance and comfort for many:

1. Spiritual Guidance: It provides

teachings and principles that guide believers in their spiritual journey and everyday life.

2. Source of Comfort: In times of trouble or uncertainty, many turn to the Bible for solace and reassurance, finding peace in its passages.

3. Connection with the Divine: The Bible is often seen as a way to understand and connect with God, offering insights into the nature of the divine and the human relationship with it.

Overall, its role as a spiritual guide and source of comfort is central to its significance in the lives of many believers.

Methods of meditation and reflection on biblical texts

The following list of methods of meditation and reflection on biblical texts is incomplete. However, this list is profitable for a high-level discussion:

1. **Lectio Divina:** (Latin for "Divine Reading") A traditional practice involving reading, meditation, prayer, and contemplation. These practices aim to study Scripture and engage with it as the living word, promoting a deeper communion with God and enhancing understanding of His teachings.

2. **Journaling:** Writing down thoughts and reflections on passages. As the

reader writes their thoughts, they process more fully the depth of what is being conveyed to them.

3. **Prayerful Reading:** Engaging with the text through prayer, seeking guidance or insights. By reading a passage and praying those words back to God, the reader learns to actively process not only the words of the Bible but the heart and intention behind the words.

4. **Group Study and Discussion:** Sharing insights and interpretations with others. By processing Scripture as a group, each individual takes advantage of the collective thoughts of the whole group.

5. **Contemplative Practices:** Using silence and solitude to reflect deeply on the meanings of texts. It is a method of digesting Scripture slowly with plenty of time to reflect without distractions.

These methods help individuals to connect more deeply with the spiritual and personal significance of the Bible. Hopefully, you see the benefit of all five approaches and are led to pursue each in your own way.

The relationship between prayer and Bible study

The relationship between prayer and Bible study is deeply intertwined. Prayer often accompanies Bible study, allowing individuals to seek understanding and connect spiritually with the text. When you mix prayer with reading the Bible, it's like having a heart-to-heart with the text. Imagine diving into a passage and then taking a moment to pray about it. This isn't just about figuring out what the words mean; it's about feeling them and letting them sink in. Through prayer, you're asking for a nudge in the right direction, a hint to understand not just with your mind but also with your heart. It's less about studying and more about connecting on a deeper level, turning Bible reading into a conversation with something bigger than yourself.

Prayer can also be a way to ask for guidance in interpreting the Bible and to reflect on its teachings. Praying while studying the Bible is like asking for a helping hand to guide you through its teachings. Imagine reading a tricky passage and figuring out what to make of it. Here's where prayer steps in. You might quietly ask for clarity, wisdom, or a new perspective. It's a way of reflecting on what you've read, mulling it over not just in your thoughts but in your spirit, too. Through this, you're seeking a deeper, more personal understanding of the Bible's messages, hoping to apply them in your life meaningfully.

Studying the Bible alongside prayer can be seen as a dialogue with God, where the text speaks to the individual, and prayer is the response. Studying the Bible with prayer is like having a two-way conversation with God. As you read the text, it's as if God is speaking to you through the words on the page, offering wisdom, comfort, or challenge. Then, when you pray, you're responding to that message.

You might express gratitude, seek further understanding, or ask how to apply what you've read. This back-and-forth creates a deeper, more personal engagement with the Bible, making it not just a book to be read but a dynamic means of communication with God.

This relationship enhances both the understanding of the Bible and the depth of one's spiritual life. Remember that relationship is God's purpose for sending us the Bible. Let's transition into how we can position ourselves to go beyond the Bible to know its Author.

Chapter Five

Connecting with God, the Author

Exploring the concept of divine inspiration in the Bible

2 Peter 1:20-21 tells us, "Above all, you must realize that no prophecy in Scripture ever came from the prophet's own understanding, or from human initiative. No, those prophets were moved by the Holy Spirit, and they spoke from God."

What does it look like to be moved by the Holy Spirit to communicate on His behalf? Exploring the concept of divine inspiration in the Bible involves understanding how it is believed that God influenced or guided the authors of the biblical texts. This belief varies among different religious traditions:

1. **Verbal Inspiration:** Some hold that God dictated the exact words of the Bible to its authors.

2. **Plenary Inspiration:** This view suggests that while the words are those of human authors, the Holy Spirit divinely guided the content or message.

3. **Dynamic Inspiration:** Here, the emphasis is on the divine influence over the ideas rather than the specific words.

Exploring divine inspiration is central to understanding the Bible's authority, interpretation, and relevance in religious contexts. However, the Bible tells us in 2 Timothy 3:16-17, "All Scripture is inspired by God and is useful to teach us what is true and to make us realize what is wrong in our lives. It corrects us when we are wrong and teaches us to do what is right. God uses it to prepare and equip His people to do every good work."

Whether you believe that God controlled every word of the writers or that He inspired the ideas they wrote about, it is critical to accept that He was involved in its creation and continuation throughout the ages. God has a vital love letter to convey, and He will effectively communicate it until the end.

How Different Faiths View the Bible's Author

Different faiths have varying views on the authorship of the Bible:

1. **Judaism:** Views the Hebrew Bible (Tanakh) as God's inspiration, with Moses and prophets as critical authors.

2. **Christianity:** Believes the entire Bible, both Old and New Testaments, is divinely inspired. Views vary on how directly God influenced the authors.

3. **Islam:** Recognizes parts of the Bible but believes the Quran is the final, unaltered word of God.

4. **Other Faiths:** Some may see the Bible

as valuable literature or contain moral truths, but not as divine revelation.

Each faith's perspective influences how they interpret and apply the Bible's teachings. The vital aspect of God's role in this process is best seen in 2 Samuel 14:14, which states:

"All of us must die eventually. Our lives are like water spilled out on the ground, which cannot be gathered up again. But God does not just sweep life away; instead, he devises ways to bring us back when we have been separated from him."

The Bible is calling to us and drawing our hearts to know the One who loves us with a love beyond anything we could ever imagine.

1 John 4:9-10 God showed how much He loved us by sending His one and only Son into

the world so that we might have eternal life through Him. (10) This is real love—not that we loved God, but that He loved us and sent His Son as a sacrifice to take away our sins.

The role of the Bible in understanding God's character and intentions

The Bible plays a central role, according to many religious traditions, in understanding God's character and intentions:

1. Revelation of God's Nature: It portrays various attributes of God, such as love, justice, mercy, and omnipotence.

2. Divine Intentions and Will: Biblical narratives and teachings reveal God's

intentions for humanity, including moral and ethical guidance.

3. Relationship with Humanity: The Bible depicts the evolving relationship between God and people, offering insights into divine expectations and human responses.

Thus, for believers, the Bible is a crucial source for comprehending the nature and desires of the heart of God. It is essential that we read Scripture with all possibilities open simultaneously so that God may speak to us about His nature, His will, and His desire for a relationship with us.

As we weave together the rich tapestry of history, the personal resonance we find in the Bible's pages, and the deep spiritual connections we've explored, we arrive at a more comprehensive understanding of this ancient yet ever-relevant text. This journey through time, self, and spirit isn't just about gathering knowledge; it's about opening doors to continuous discovery and reflection. As we turn the page to the next chapter, we invite you to keep this spirit of inquiry alive. Let's step to the conclusion.

Chapter Six

Conclusion: The Endless Journey

Throughout this book, we have explored the roots and rich history of the Bible. We have analyzed how the Bible is relevant in modern times and can be interpreted on several simultaneous levels to understand it more fully. Finally, we have seen how the Bible is a spiritual guidebook that connects us with the Author, God Himself. How do you personally feel directed to respond, considering these themes?

Remember that the ongoing relevance of the Bible in the reader's life is multifaceted:

1. **Moral and Ethical Guidance:** The Bible offers timeless principles for ethical living and moral decision-making.

2. **Spiritual Growth:** It serves as a source for spiritual reflection, growth, and connection with God.

3. **Cultural and Historical Insight:** As a foundational text, the Bible provides insights into human history, culture, and psychology.

4. **Personal Resonance:** Many find personal comfort, inspiration, and answers to life's questions in its

teachings.

5. **Community and Identity:** For religious communities, it's a central text that shapes communal practices and individual identities.

So, the Bible plays a vital role in people's lives worldwide. It is more than just words on paper; it resonates in many ways with many people, regardless of culture, background, or political environment. Jeremiah 31:3 reminds us, "Long ago the LORD said... "I have loved you, My people, with an everlasting love. With unfailing love, I have drawn you to Myself."

Drawing from the rich tapestry of the Bible as a living and dynamic text, I challenge you to embark on your own journey of exploration. Delve into its pages, not just as ancient

Scripture but as a vibrant source of inspiration and guidance. Let the Bible's diverse narratives and teachings resonate with your personal experiences, challenge your perspectives, and inspire your thoughts. Whether through the lens of faith, literature, history, or moral philosophy, discover your unique path of understanding and connection. Let the Bible be more than a book on your shelf; let it lead you to the dynamic presence of God's Spirit in your life, continuously engaging and shaping your understanding of the world and yourself.

The journey through the Bible is one that never truly ends. Each reading and each reflection brings new insights, challenges our perspectives, and deepens our understanding. As you continue to explore its pages, remember that the Bible is not just a historical artifact or a collection of ancient texts; it is a living, breathing source of wisdom, comfort, and inspiration.

I encourage you to approach your study with an open heart and mind. Let the stories and teachings of the Bible speak to you in new ways. Engage with different interpretations and perspectives to enrich your understanding. Whether you study it for personal growth, spiritual depth, or intellectual curiosity, the Bible offers endless opportunities for exploration and discovery.

Keep asking questions, seeking answers, and finding personal meaning in its words. Your journey through the Bible is personal, and each step can lead to profound insights about the world, faith, and yourself. So, continue to read, reflect, and learn. The Bible's wisdom is timeless, and its lessons are always relevant, providing guidance and perspective for every generation.

Please Leave a Review

Dear Reader,

I hope this message finds you well. I kindly request your honest review of my recent book, "What is the Bible?: Understand Its History, Find Personal Meaning, and Connect With Its Author" Your opinion is incredibly valuable to me, and I would be grateful for your candid thoughts and feedback. Your insights could be tremendously helpful to other potential readers in understanding what to expect from the book.

Thank you for considering my request, and I look forward to potentially hearing your thoughts on my work.

Warm regards, Jack Wolf

Endnotes

1. Academic, Z. (2019, June 19). *The history of the Bible. Zondervan Academic.* https://zondervanacademic.com/blog/the-history-of-the-bible

2. The Bible. (2018, January 19). *HISTORY.* https://www.history.com/topics/religion/bible#sources

3. *Bible: New Living Translation.* (2016). NLT Online. https://www.tyndale.com/nlt/

4. *The role of Bible History in shaping Western civilization - Bible History.* (n.d.). https://bible-history.com/news/the-role -of-bible-history-in-shaping-western-civi lization

5. *Remembering God's smuggler, Brother Andrew.* (n.d.). Frontline Fellowship. https://www.frontlinemissionsa.org/in- memorium/remembering-gods-smuggle r-brother-andrew